Intuitive Love Tarot

Get Guidance & Answers on Dating, Marriage,

Soulmates, Breakups, & More.

By

Kelly Wallace

Professional Psychic Counselor

DrKellyPsychic.com[1]

---

1. http://DrKellyPsychic.com/

Table of Contents

Books by Kelly Wallace

10 Minutes A Day to A Powerful New Life

Become Your Higher Self – Using Spiritual Energy to Transform Your Life

Breaking The Worry Habit – Stop Your Anxious Thoughts And Start Living!

Chakras – Heal, Clear, And Strengthen Your Energy Centers

Clear Your Karma – The Healing Power of Your Past Lives

Contacting Your Spirit Guides – Meeting and Working with Your Invisible Helpers

Creating A Charmed Life – Enchantments to Attract, Repel, Cleanse & Heal

Dream Work – Using The Wisdom Of Your Sleeping Mind To Change Your Waking Life

Energy Work – Heal, Cleanse, and Strengthen Your Aura

Everyday Miracles – Powerful Steps to Wonderful Experiences

Finding Your Life Purpose – Uncover Your Soul's True Goals

Healing the Child Within – Rewrite Your Early Childhood Life Script

How to Cure Candida – Yeast Infection Symptoms, Causes, Diet & Natural Remedies

Imposter Syndrome – Breaking Free and Finding Your Confidence

Intuitive Living – Developing Your Psychic Gifts

Intuitive Tarot – Learn the Tarot Instantly

Intuitive Love Tarot - Get Guidance & Answers on Dating, Marriage,

Soulmates, Breakups, & More.

Is He The One? Finding And Keeping Your Soulmate

Master the Art of Picking Up Women

Master the Art of Dating Women

Master the Art of Sex and Seduction

Never Good Enough – Escaping The Prison Of Perfectionism

No-Sweat Homeschooling – The Cheap, Free, and Low-Stress Way to Teach Your Kids

Psychic Vampires – Protect and Heal Yourself from Energy Predators

Reclaiming Your Soul – Healing Your Spirit, Building Confidence, Finding Your Voice

Reprogram Your Subconscious – Use The Power Of Your Mind

Shadow Work Book 1 – Understanding And Making Peace With Your Darker Side

Shadow Work Book 2 – Facing and Embracing the Dark Side of Your Soul

Signs From The Universe – How To Recognize And Interpret These Life-Changing Messages

Spirit Guides And Healing Energy – Worth Your Guides, Aura, and Chakras

Spirits I Have Known – Haunted Places, Haunted People

Spiritual Alchemy – Transform Your Life and Everyone In It

The Art Of Happiness – Living A Life Of Peace And Simplicity

The Love You Deserve – Release Toxic Relationships and Attract Your Soulmate

The Mended Soul – Healing Your Mind, Body, & Spirit From Anxiety & Depression

The Overwhelmed Empath – A Guide For Sensitive Souls

The Power of Pets – How to Psychically Communicate with Your Pet

Transforming Your Money Mindset – From Broke To Abundance

True Wealth – Reprogram Your Subconscious for Financial Success

About Kelly Wallace

Kelly is a bestselling spiritual and self-help author, former radio show host, and has been a professional psychic counselor for over twenty years. She can see, hear, sense, and feel information sent from Spirit, the Universe, and a client's Higher Self.

Whether your problems or concerns center on love, finances, family, career, health, education, or your purpose in life, she writes books that will help you easily make lasting changes.

Kelly also offers professional psychic counseling, caring guidance, and solutions that work! More than just a typical psychic reading or counseling session, you will feel you've found a real friend during your time of need—whether you simply want answers and guidance to your current worries or concerns, or you're interested in learning more about your soulmate, spirit guides, angels, past lives, or anything else.

Contact her today for an in-depth and life-altering reading!

Website: DrKellyPsychic.com[1]

Email: Dr.Kelly.Psychic.Counselor@gmail.com

---

1. http://psychicreadingsbydrkelly.webs.com/

What This Book Covers

Introduction

Whether you're at a crossroads in your current relationship, are trying to find your soulmate, are wondering what lessons you and your partner need to learn, or are just in need of some guidance and direction, the tarot can help. I've been doing Love Readings for decades now and I'm always surprised, enlightened, and, yes, sometimes confused by what the cards are trying to relay.

One thing I can say for certain though is at some point in the future I can always look back and say, "Oh, so that's what the tarot cards were trying to tell me!" More often than not though, the messages are clear, even if we don't always like the answers. Yes, the cards are always honest! What's really great about them is that you can get instant answers to your questions, as well as advice on what to embrace and what to be wary of in any relationship.

Are they truly accurate though?

After all, how can a deck of cards, one that you can order online or pick up off a shelf in any metaphysical shop, really know about you and your partner—past, present, and future? Honestly, the cards themselves don't hold any magic or psychic powers, they're simply a tool that uses symbols and imagery to help unlock your subconscious and tap into your higher, wiser self. You actually have all of the knowledge and answers inside you at this very moment, but the accuracy of your readings depends on your intention and your openness to see the truth in the cards.

But what if you've never read the tarot before?

Or what if you've only worked with your cards for a short while or are uncertain about the meanings? The first book I wrote about reading the tarot: *Intuitive Tarot – Read the Cards Instantly* has been one of my strongest sellers over the years. I've gotten so many emails from readers who had never touched a tarot deck before or had struggled to memorize traditional meanings, telling me that trusting their intuition while doing readings helped them so much. In this book, I'll cover how to use your intuition so you can do *Love Readings* for yourself or even others. (I offer traditional meanings at the end of the book too, just to offer a bit more guidance.)

Something I love about the tarot is that no two people will see the cards in the same way. That's why tapping into your intuition is so important. Yes, you're going to interpret the cards based on your current hopes and fears, your past and present, but as you go even deeper you'll reach your very soul where all of the guidance you need now or ever will need is waiting to be unlocked.

The Best Tool For Matters Of The Heart

We all need direction and guidance at times in life, especially when it comes to relationships. The cards will show you, without bias, where you're doing well, where you need to work on things, what's holding you back, and so much more. In fact, the tarot can help you unlock just about any answer you're looking for.

Another thing that I really love about the cards is you don't simply get yes or no answers. You're presented with a whole range of symbols, scenes, colors, and numbers that offer details to help you find your way. Think of it as having a loving yet straightforward counselor in a box.

It's true though that very often we'll see what we want to see in the cards, be it positive or negative. You might interpret the card or cards one way and when the situation has come to pass you see that things turn out differently than what you had interpreted at first, and that's okay! Hindsight is 20/20 and it's how we learn and grow, right? And, that's why it's important to allow your intuition to take the driver's seat, but we'll get into that a bit later.

Tarot is a key that helps to unlock the things you already know but either you aren't fully aware of or don't want to acknowledge just yet. My view is, if you're asking a question it's because you already know the answer. The cards simply help to bring that information to light. Whether you accept or deny the guidance depends on how you're currently feeling.

You and your closest friend could sit down with the same deck of cards and ask the same question and you would both get different messages. That's because you're seeing the cards through your energy, reading them with your intentions, using your own unique experiences in life, and your personal intuition. You'll then see the symbols in the cards that will make perfect sense whether now or in the near future.

FAQs About Tarot

Once you start using the tarot more often you'll see just how helpful it is in uncovering both the seen and unseen aspects of your life. Right now, you might have questions regarding these cards so let's cover some things people have asked me about over the years.

1. Can the tarot really be useful?

Yes! The cards can give you instant answers to your questions, help you to better understand yourself and others, as well as strengthening your intuition and perception. You'll find that you're more open to things you normally wouldn't have seen or have ignored, as well as noticing more help and guidance sent from the Universe. They're an excellent tool for personal growth—mentally, emotionally, and spiritually.

2. What can the tarot do and not do?

The tarot can:

- Open your mind to new ways of thinking and seeing things

- Offer direction and guidance

- Help with personal growth and healing

- Give insight into why others are behaving in certain ways

- Show you where and how you can make changes

- Help you to make informed choices

- Help you to feel more empowered

The tarot can't:

- Predict death

- Force you to do something

- Give exact dates or absolute outcomes

- Do everything for you

- Work magic, create miracles, or inflict curses

3. Which tarot deck is the best?

Whatever deck you feel drawn to is the best deck for you. I suggest having two or three decks that you can go between when doing your readings. Sometimes I'll get tired of one deck and reach for a different one I have.

When choosing a deck, search online and look at them beforehand. Some don't have pictures for the Minor Arcana cards and are much more like a regular deck of playing cards. These decks would just have 1-10 cups, wands, swords, and pentacles rather than actual scenes and symbols. You want your deck to be rich in symbolism. This is very important for the most helpful and accurate readings.

If you still aren't sure which to choose just yet, a few good decks to start with would be the Rider-Waite, Gilded, Morgan Greer, or Connolly. The Connolly deck is good for those who feel nervous about cards such as The Devil and Death. This deck has replaced them with "Materialism" and "Transformation", and is the first deck I bought when starting on my tarot journey. More than two decades later, I still use these cards quite often.

I've also had clients ask me if more expensive decks are better than cheaper ones. I've found no difference whatsoever in a deck I spent $10 on compared to the ones I've spent triple or more on. I mostly focus on card decks that appeal to me and seem to draw me into the themes and designs.

4. What should I do with my cards when I first get them?

When you've bought a new deck, whether you're totally new to tarot or have been doing readings for a while, I always suggest imbuing the cards with your energy as soon as possible. Just take your deck out of the pack, place the cards face down on the floor, bed, or table, spread them out, and stir them up for a minute or two. Afterward, scoop the cards up into a deck again and shuffle them at least three times as you do normal playing cards.

You don't have to do any formal ritual, though some people like to light candles or incense and spend a few minutes relaxing or meditating before shuffling their cards just to be sure they're in the right frame of mind.

You can then put them back into the original box, or something a little more special like putting them in a fabric bag, wrapping them in cloth, or placing them in a wooden box.

In just a bit we'll cover ways to get to know your cards better.

5. Do I need to be psychic to read tarot cards?

I always say that everyone is psychic to one degree or another, and *everyone* is intuitive. But what's the difference? Intuition is more of a gut feeling you get when something is about to happen or if something or someone just seems "not right". We often say we got bad vibes, and that's exactly what it is. Your intuition is picking up on this energy.

I've read articles stating that all humans have intuition and we developed it eons ago as a way of self-preservation. We needed to keep ourselves safe, our tribe or clan safe, so we would instinctively pick up on negative energy to protect and warn the people closest to us. It's more of a survival instinct, which is incredibly helpful.

When one is psychic it's like having a "knowing", as if the information is automatically imprinted in your mind. More than just a feeling, you might see pictures or snippets much like a movie in your mind's eye, hear words, and more. Sometimes this might pertain to something or someone negative you're already involved with, but very often you get this information about complete strangers or things that are unknown or seem ordinary. Even so, it's different than intuition which is more like a hunch.

Intuition can develop into psychic abilities though and the tarot is a great tool to hone this gift. The cards can help you to take your normal intuition and fine-tune it, making the information and predictions more precise and accurate. In time, you'll be able to see, hear, and feel these messages rather than just relying on those gut feelings. It's like going from trying to capture a puff of smoke to being able to grasp and hold something much more concrete.

Tapping Into Your Intuition

I'm always amazed at how accurate tarot cards are. I got my first deck in the mid-90s. It was the Connolly Tarot and I loved the rich symbolism on every one of the cards. I also liked that it didn't have the Devil or Death cards since, back then, I was still so new to tarot and a little worried about getting either of those in a reading.

Feeling eager, I went home, shuffled the deck, thought of a question, and laid three cards out. I then used the book that came with the deck and I felt that it was somewhat accurate, which still amazed me, but the definitions, at least to me, seemed generic. Since I had my journal near me, I opened it up and took a good look at the cards I had drawn. I then asked myself what, if anything, they meant to me personally. What resonated with me in those colorful cardboard rectangles?

Once I got that all written down I looked my words over again, looked at the cards, and compared it with my original question. Now the reading made more sense to me! It was personal and I could really see my life, people I knew, experiences in my life, my obstacles or problems, dreams or goals, right there in the cards. And the best thing about it was that it was so easy.

When I first got my deck I felt a little stressed wondering if I'd ever be able to remember all of the traditional meanings for the cards. After all, there are 78 of them, and if you also read reversed cards that's 156 different messages. Not only that, but each card has several definitions. It can feel overwhelming, to say the least.

There are a few ways you can learn to read the tarot intuitively.

1. Getting Familiar

I do this exercise with every new deck I get, even though I've been reading the tarot for decades now. Every deck will have its own imagery and energy.

After shuffling your cards well, set the deck near you and take the top card. Look at it for a moment and pay attention to how it makes you feel. What are the first thoughts or emotions that come to you? Are you drawn to any of the colors, the scene itself, the figure on the card, or anything else? Or, does anything on the card repel you, making you feel nervous, angry, fearful, or confused? Although there are truly no "bad" cards, depending on what's going on in your life now and in the past can dictate how you feel about certain cards.

Also, as you go through each card you can look up the traditional meanings and see what you think about them. Or, better yet, use a new journal to keep your tarot notes in, list the cards you draw, and what your initial reactions to them are. You won't be wrong, trust me. I'm not saying that traditional meanings are worthless, and they can offer insight if you're completely uncertain about a card. However, I'm a firm believer in trusting our intuition.

You're a unique individual, just like everyone else on this planet, and no two people have been through the same situations. It just makes sense that you're going to see something different in the cards than another person would and this is especially helpful when reading for yourself.

Although I've been reading the tarot for many years now I'm always amazed at something new I find each time I look at my cards. In fact, no two readings are ever alike because, depending on my question, current circumstances, or goals, different things on the card call my attention.

2. Three Card Reading

I know we're at the beginning of the book, but let's jump right in with a reading. I want you to get used to your cards and how they feel to you. Trust me, there are no wrong answers. Just let your imagination and intuition guide you through this.

After shuffling your deck, get out a journal and a pen, think of a question you'd like the answer to, and lay out three cards. Write down the date you're doing the reading and what cards you drew. You can choose the first three cards off the top of the deck or spread the deck out in front of you and choose three cards at random. When forming your question, make sure that it's open-ended, rather than something that can have a simple yes or no answer.

Look over the cards and see how anything in them can pertain to your current question. What grabs your attention first? Is it the person or animal in the card? If so, what does their mood or energy seem like? What are they doing? Maybe a color pops out at you. What does this color represent to you?

Just look them over and write down all of your thoughts. If the cards could talk, what would they say to you? Here you're using your feelings, thoughts, and intuition to read the cards rather than just trying to find the meaning.

3. Write a short story.

This time, choose a card at random, or go through the deck and choose a card that captures your attention. In your journal or a separate notebook, put the name of the card at the top and just let your imagination create a story centered on it. Don't think too hard and just go with your first instincts.

Over the years, I've gotten longer stories, very short ones, just a paragraph, or even a thoughtful sentence. I've written stories that were sad, scary, funny, or thought-provoking. Some cards I felt absolutely no attachment to. Over time I realized it was because my subconscious wasn't ready to deal with whatever issue it represented at the moment or it just didn't pertain at the time being.

You could even take this exercise a bit further and choose three cards so your story has a beginning, middle, and end.

4. Who, what, when, where, why?

As with the other exercises, either pick a card at random or look through the deck and choose one that catches your attention. Either out loud or in your mind, have a conversation with the card. If there's a figure on it, ask who they are and what they're doing there or what they're seeking. When did they get there, where are they going, and why? You can also write this conversation in your journal if you'd like.

5. The morning card.

Before you start your day, choose a card at random and look it over. Don't spend too much time on it, just pay attention to what's on the card, the scene, colors, etc. At the end of your day before going to bed, look at the card again and see if anything in the card appeared throughout your day. Maybe you interacted with someone who looked like the figure in the card, or perhaps one of the colors in the card really stood out to you and something during the day was that same color.

It might sound simple, but if you use your intuition each time you do a reading you'll gain more confidence and your readings will become even more accurate. All of this wonderful guidance is at your fingertips and can not only help you personally, but everyone in your life as well.

Yes, traditional meanings can be useful, so definitely read up on them. At the end of this book, I give some common definitions for each of the 78 cards. This way, you can compare the cards you drew to traditional meanings, but never doubt your own instincts when doing a reading, especially if it's for yourself.

My Favorite 3-Card Spreads

Although I often do longer readings, three-card spreads are the ones I prefer. They're quick readings that easily get to the heart of the matter without overwhelming me with too much information. And, if I do want more guidance and want to dig in further, I just pull more cards when I'm done reading the first three.

Before shuffling and laying out the cards, I decide on what I would like guidance on. Sometimes I want information on a pattern I keep repeating, or to get an overview of some potential choices or opportunities. Sometimes I'm not even sure about what I'm looking for. In those cases, I just leave my mind open and trust my intuition and the information I see in the cards.

Some of my favorite three-card spreads are:

- Past, Present, Future

This reading is useful whether you're trying to solve childhood issues, figure out how you're doing now compared to the past and how the future might look, lessons you needed to learn then, now, and in the future, and so on. Anything or anyone you would like a longer time frame of information on can be included in this reading. I've used it to look at something as early as last week, to things decades ago.

A while back, I used this spread to see where I was a few years ago, where I was now, and where I could possibly be in the future. Of course, the outcome would rely on what I did or didn't do to create any potential changes. Another time I wanted to see if I was choosing different types of relationships. I saw that nothing had changed, unfortunately, so I knew I needed to do some internal speculation and healing.

- Choice A, B, C

This is self-explanatory. If you have three choices and want to see what or whom could potentially be the best, this is a good reading. If you don't have three choices, you could always use the third card as the potential outcome or a message of guidance from the cards and your higher self.

Years ago I used this spread because I was talking to three men on a dating site. They all seemed nice and interested in me, though I knew that online interactions were far different than in person. So, I asked the cards to just give me a bit of information about each of these men. I made my notes and honestly decided to go out with all three of them. After all, I didn't want to put my love life solely in the hands of my tarot cards.

Sure enough, the reading was correct. I won't get into all of the details, but the notes I had were: Guy A – Could have a potential anger problem or be overly sexual. Guy B – Probably out of work now or is frequently. Guy C – Honest and kind, but not ready to date just yet.

- Me, Other Person, Obstacle or Possible Outcome

I can't tell you how many times I've used this spread when it comes to every relationship in my life—whether friends, family, or romantic partners. It doesn't matter who is in your life now or who comes into your life, you're both individuals and there's going to be friction from time to time.

Reading the cards in this way gives me a better idea of where I'm coming from, where the other person stands or what they might be dealing with, and how we can work through our differences to strengthen and support each other and the relationship.

And, yes, sometimes you'll learn if you should just let go, whether temporarily or permanently. That was a lesson I learned when doing this reading while in a short-term relationship. When I first met this man we hit it off right away. Everything seemed to click into place and the chemistry was out of this world.

Fast forward three months later and things fizzled out seemingly overnight. I pulled three cards: one for me, one for him, and one representing a possible outcome. Trust me, the cards will not sugarcoat things. I saw in the images that I was giving far too much, he wasn't ready for anything long-term, and parting ways would be the best solution.

Of course, I didn't heed the guidance and still tried making things work for a few more months until we finally ended things. If I had listened to the messages of the tarot (my higher self) I would have saved myself both time and heartache.

- Strength, Weakness, Solution

This spread came in really handy before I ventured out into the dating world again, but it's useful at any point in life when you want to focus internally and how you can work on shortcomings and fortify your positive attributes. The final card can offer valuable insight into how to work on things.

I'm a giver at heart and always want to help others. The first card showed this, and I felt pretty good seeing it. Then I turned over the next card and it showed that I had a tendency to give far too much until I was completely drained to the core, annoyed everyone by being far too helpful, or ended up feeling resentful. I cringed a little when I admitted that it was true. The final card offered some helpful advice, reminding me to offer help when someone asked and not to just jump up and solve everything for them.

- Who, What, Why (usually a lesson to be learned)

In this book, I'm mainly focusing on romantic relationships, but any of these spreads can be used for other types of relationships: friends, family, coworkers, etc. This particular spread helped to shed some light on some patterns I follow.

When I laid out the first card there was a female on it and right away she reminded me of my mother. So, I knew this particular issue involved her. The next card showed a depressed man at a table with five cups of wine around him. To me, this represented her addictions and depression.

The final card, the lesson to be learned, was difficult for me to fully embrace at the time. But, now that so many years have passed, I realize the advice from the cards/my higher self/my intuition was correct. I needed to release everything, release my negative feelings towards her, and take that weight off my shoulders. Carrying around animosity and trying to be absolutely perfect wasn't allowing my soul to shine through as brightly as I wanted it to. Although it took many years, doing that one simple reading at least pointed me in the direction my healing needed to go.

- Me, Happenings, Possible Outcome.

I've used this spread before going out on dates or job interviews. I also use this as a daily spread, sort of like a daily horoscope. The cards can show people or situations you might encounter, and how it might all turn out. It's great to get a snapshot of potential events—whether positive or negative.

Just like with the morning one-card reading, pull three cards, look them over, and keep this information in mind. At the end of the event, look them over and see what meshes. And, oftentimes, it can warn you against something or someone, or propel you forward. Always follow your instincts.

There are so many ways you can do a three-card reading. Sometimes though I just want to see what the cards have to share with me and I won't put any label on them. Maybe I'll just ask a question such as, "What can I do to get over this current obstacle in my life?" Then I'll name the obstacle and envision it in my mind as I shuffle the cards and lay them out. I'll then look them over as a whole, and one-by-one to see what they want to tell me.

I've avoided some potentially negative outcomes by following the information the cards offered. Other times, I was uncertain but the cards seemed positive, so I took a chance and was pleasantly surprised. Very often we get in our own way. The tarot can help clear away some of the clouds in our minds.

Pay Attention To Patterns

Right now you might be feeling a little overwhelmed. I don't want to bombard you with too much information, but I also want to include as much help as possible. Don't worry, the more you do readings, the easier it gets. Soon, everything will be second nature.

Whenever you do a reading, whether you're using three cards or a dozen or more, keep your eyes open for any patterns. Look for repeating colors, symbols, images, actions, numbers, suits, etc. because it's important.

- Repeating numbers.

For the most part, I tend to read numbers as time-frames. For example, let's say I do a spread and see that there's one particular number that showed up more than any others. I'll often interpret this to mean weeks or months when something can potentially take place. Typically, I don't read any numbers to mean years because so much can change—or stay the same. I also don't read numbers as days very often because the time range is too short. You need to give yourself and the Universe a little time to work on things, especially if others are involved.

Numbers also have their own meanings such as balance, creativity, communication, and so much more. I've included information on numbers and the messages they carry at the back of the book. It's not an exhaustive list by any means, but can give you some guidance as to what the particular number can be telling you. Of course, there are many books and websites dedicated to numerology that go into detail, so feel free to do some more exploring on your own.

Recently, a client of mine bought a tarot reading from me and she wanted to know about her new relationship. I laid out three cards and then got a strange feeling because all three of the cards were 3s. What are the odds?

My first thought was that her new boyfriend wasn't being honest and was cheating. I set my knee-jerk reaction aside though and looked deeper into the cards while laying out five more and saw that any females that did come up seemed older. I asked her if he was close to his mother (thinking that she could be a potential obstacle) and sure enough, his mother was a huge wedge between them. We discussed ways to work through the situation and all the while I was thinking, "The cards were right again!"

- Repeating people.

When laying out your cards and you notice there are images of people that seem similar—all one sex, or more of one than the other, or more young adults—this can point to the problem or solution.

One time I did a reading for a client about her marriage. She had been with this man for nearly a decade and they were the best of friends, but there was not much intimacy. When I drew her cards almost all of them had a man in the scene. She assured me that she had never been unfaithful, but this male energy was coming from somewhere. Her father? Brother? Friend?

She also asked for a past life reading and I saw her in her most recent past lives as a male and I shared this with her. My intuition told me that there was more to this story but I work with my clients to find solutions rather than blurting everything out. She then admitted that she had always wondered if she was a lesbian. She had a talk with her husband that night and he said he had wondered the same thing. Five years later, she is divorced from her husband and happily married to her female soulmate.

Another time I was doing a reading, just asking the tarot to point out anything I needed to know or work on at the moment, and I kept getting cards with young girls on them. I couldn't figure that out, though I knew it was important. So, I let the reading sit in my mind for a bit. As I was making dinner that evening my mind wandered over to one of my daughters and I thought again about how closed off she'd been the past few days.

I decided to talk to her (again) and she admitted that she and her best friend had gotten into an argument and that they hadn't talked in days. My daughter is stubborn and didn't want to extend the proverbial olive branch but I asked if her friendship meant more to her than her ego. She admitted that it did and she called her friend. It was tense for a few moments, but they patched things up, cried, and were best friends again.

- The Presence of Major Arcana.

These are the first 22 cards of the tarot and represent bigger things in life, those soul lessons, while the remaining 56 are more related to daily events and lesser situations. Let's say you lay out three cards and at least two are Major Arcana. Even if you lay out ten cards and four are Major Arcana, that's still a lot when you consider the ratio of Major Arcana compared to Minor Arcana in the deck. Even if you only get one in your spread, it's still important.

What this can point to is that you might be in the midst of or coming up on a time of major changes, disruption in your life, soul lessons, karmic issues, or strong emotions. Don't worry, it's not always bad, and typically change is for the better, but with the Major Arcana the events and lessons are more intense than with any of the Minor Arcana cards. You don't need to be afraid. Just be prepared, open-minded, and willing to make changes when necessary.

- Personal associations or cues.

As you get more accustomed to reading your cards you'll no doubt start noticing that certain cards turn up for you and become personal symbols to get your attention. For instance, I often get the 7 of Pentacles which usually shows a farmer with gold coins. Whenever that card comes up, especially if it seems to have nothing to do with the subject of the reading, I know it represents work. I've either been working too hard or, on the rare occasion, slacking off. So, I realize it's a personal message to find more balance.

- Always look for guidance.

The tarot and your intuition go hand-in-hand, and your higher self is wise beyond your current years. It's that wisdom you want to bring to the surface rather than having a set of rules and a detailed road map to follow. Or, worse yet, just looking for simple yes or no answers. Also, remember that the tarot can't tell you what to do or force you to do anything, it's meant to help you make better decisions and positive changes.

A close friend of mine had recently separated from her boyfriend and she wanted nothing more than to get back together with him. She would do countless tarot readings a day, hoping to get the answers she wanted rather than the guidance she needed. Whether they would get back together or not was uncertain, but her higher self and the cards had so much to tell her about how to be a better person and how to interact more positively as a couple.

She had no desire to work on herself or the problems that had been building between them though. Instead, she simply had this intense need to be with him again regardless. I told her that even if they got back together right this very moment, all of those problems would still be there and they'd simply part ways again. She couldn't hear me though, and she certainly couldn't see the wisdom in the tarot.

Long story short, she did everything in her power to win him back (except making the necessary changes), and they tried again. Naturally, they had the same problems, and the same results, and she was left nursing a broken heart a second time.

When reading the tarot it's important to keep your eyes open for messages and patterns, your mind open to guidance and truth, and your heart open to change and healing.

The Tarot Can Help You Find Love

If you're tired of being alone or settling for relationships that are short-lived or nothing as you'd hoped they would be, know that the tarot can help transform your love life. If you're serious about uncovering your true spiritual potential and finding your soulmate, the cards can guide you to the life you desire and deserve.

Between the wisdom of your higher self and your deck of cards, you have two inspiring and enlightening tools on your side. Let's look at a couple of ways the tarot can assist you in finding your spiritual soulmate(s).

Obstacles that are in your way

There's rarely a person who wants to believe or admit that they self-sabotage so many things in their lives, especially relationships. Due to early childhood programming, past life influences, and other factors, we subconsciously set ourselves up for failure so it fits into the life script we already know. Following what you've learned and have always been doing is far easier than making healthy changes and doing something completely new.

We're creatures of habit and it's hard to make changes. But, unless you open yourself up to the reality that you're the one in charge of your destiny, you won't find long-term happiness in love or life.

Even if you feel you're aware of your patterns and trauma, even if you think this new partner is far different from anyone in your past, you still have blockages and habits that are running the show. Soon, anger, resentment, jealousy, and fear of abandonment take over. The relationship dies, and you're left feeling lonely, rejected, and isolated yet again.

Since the tarot is a spiritual and symbolic tool, it's an excellent way to grab your attention and have you see the reality of your life in all aspects. It can show you how you behave and why, the reasons you choose certain partners, and the patterns you keep repeating that sabotage even your best efforts to find true and lasting love. The cards can help you to see your challenges and how to overcome them.

Recognizing your perfect partner

By using your cards you can find out, through symbolic messages of guidance, what your ideal partner can offer you in your day-to-day life. Sure, we all have an image in our minds of what our soulmates will look like and how we'll feel when with them, but true love is far more than that.

So many people think that once they find their soulmate life will be one smooth and happy day after another. While a positive union can indeed be wonderful most days, you're two separate people making a life together. You have your own personalities and moods, past experiences, dreams, and goals. There will be times when you butt heads, argue, or feel a bit distant from one another. In a healthy relationship though, the two of you will work through things only to become stronger, and happier, and to help one another heal where and when needed.

One thing I want to mention is that everyone is brought into our lives so that either we, they, or both of you, can learn something. Oftentimes, when the lesson is learned, or if you need another "teacher", the relationship ends and someone new comes into the picture. This will repeat itself until you finally mend the wounded part of yourself that keeps attracting the seemingly wrong type of partner.

Tarot readings can show you what you've been doing wrong, how to correct it, and what to look for in your next (and best!) relationship. Your ideal partner won't fall in your lap so you'll need to do some work, but finding your soulmate is definitely in the cards.

The Tarot Can Help You To Gain Insight

You've been there before. You know the feelings. A relationship starts out so wonderful and magical. The two of you connect like nobody you've known before, and you believe that finally, at long last, this is "the one". Then, weeks, months, or years go by and real life creeps in. Your insecurities and traumas resurface, and so do theirs, and then everything falls apart.

Every time you go through this it can have you holding on to the other person with superhuman strength (which only seems to make things worse), or calling it quits and walking away before the relationship degrades even more—because you know it will.

A lot of people aren't even aware of when, where, and why their relationship started turning cold and ugly. Others are aware of what causes the issues but they don't know how to fix them. That's where your tarot cards can help. They can reveal new ways to approach your relationship(s), and remind you of what things you need to work on and where you need to heal and become stronger. They're amazing at offering the insight one needs to make important relationships work and flourish.

How the tarot can help improve your love life

When you're in a relationship it's so easy to get caught up in everything and let it overwhelm you. Whether it's small daily things, or a bigger obstacle you've encountered with them, the tarot can help you take a mental step back so you can see things more clearly. You can also get a glimpse into how your partner may be feeling and their point of view on things so you can better understand them and their actions.

Friends and family all give their well-meaning advice and opinions, but this is always biased since they care about you. The tarot is an impartial counselor, showing you the truth and how you can make the best choices for a happier life and love.

I've used the tarot countless times for various relationships in my life, whether romantic or platonic, and if there's one thing I can warn you about it's to get comfortable with being uncomfortable. You are going to be faced with things that you either never admitted to yourself or keep pushing to the back of your mind so you don't have to deal with it. As I mentioned, the cards are incredibly honest and you will see where you falter and why, the truth about various relationships, and so much more.

The first time I did a reading for myself on a very dysfunctional relationship, believing it was all the other person, the cards let me know my role in everything too. All I could do for a moment was to sit back and say "Yikes". As the saying goes, all relationships are 50/50. To think that you're just choosing the wrong people and are the victim or that you have absolutely no role in things is false.

I'll admit, it was a pretty hard pill to swallow when I saw my actions and habits glaring back at me from the cards. But, it was also freeing in a way. It felt good to know that I could learn, heal, and grow. That I could, eventually, attract a positive life partner rather than every other relationship I'd dealt with up to that point. I can't control anyone else, and I shouldn't even try, but I can control my own actions and reactions. I can learn from the past and make my future better.

I was so used to just letting my past and my insecurities take the wheel and go wherever they wanted to. It was eye-opening and a bit exhilarating to know that I could actually make changes and get my love life going in a different direction from that moment on.

The cards are excellent for bringing to the surface all of those thoughts and emotions you've been repressing for years or even decades. It doesn't matter if you're using the tarot to focus on a relationship you were in many years ago, or one you might be in right now, it will show you what you need to know.

Maybe you lost respect for your partner, maybe they don't work, have an addiction, aren't affectionate, have cheated, or for some reason, you're just losing interest. A reading with your cards will show you the truth, even if it's uncomfortable or unflattering, so you can face your fears, overcome any denial, and finally work through it.

Keep in mind that the cards aren't going to tell you what to do. Instead, they will offer clues, through their rich symbolism, and suggest a course of action for you to take and what you can do for the best possible outcome. The rest is up to you and how you perceive the messages.

You might have to do a few readings over the course of time until your mind can set aside the denial or defensiveness so you can ultimately find the courage to take action and make decisions that are for your own highest good.

Don't be surprised if you aren't ready to hear the truth right away. I know I wasn't. One time I did a reading for one of my relationships and it told me what I already knew in my mind and heart but didn't want to accept. My partner had a drinking problem and was emotionally immature, nothing would change, and my best bet was to break things off before they got even more toxic.

Of course, I didn't listen and stayed much longer than I should have. Not until we were both absolutely miserable and I saw not one shred of hope for the future did I finally leave. I could have saved myself so much time and heartache if I had been honest with myself when the cards showed me what I needed to know.

Another thing a reading can do is suggest a few possible paths you could take. As I mentioned in the three-card spreads earlier, a really good one to use is: Path A, Path B, and Possible Outcome. I would often do this to see if the tarot had a few suggestions for a positive outcome, or if I stayed the course or changed courses how things might work out. It can warn you if a certain plan you have might not work out well, and if there might be a better route to the greatest good.

Not just for romantic relationships

The main focus of this book is on romantic partnerships, but as I mentioned a bit before, the tarot can also help you improve all relationships in your life. You might have been arguing with one of your parents or teenage children, a coworker has been particularly difficult lately, or a close friendship seems to be drifting apart.

The tarot can give you a glimpse into the other person's motives, fears, and thoughts. It can advise you on how best to deal with the people you're having conflicts with. It can help you pinpoint the problems and where they stem from so you can take action to mend things, if possible. It can also help you to be more aware of how to handle certain people and situations.

In the end, the decisions are yours to make. Just because the tarot and your higher self offer suggestions doesn't mean you're ready, willing, or able to follow through on things. I can't count how many times I did a reading and said to myself, "Yeah, yeah, I know this, but I'm just not ready." And you know that? That's okay! We learn and grow at our own pace. When you're ready things will click into place and will make more sense and, hopefully, be easier.

Something to always keep in mind when doing a reading is to be honest. You won't get any benefit from the tarot if you're denying something or feel too angry or embarrassed to admit the truth. You need to be as relaxed as possible and have a clear vision of your relationship and your ultimate goal so you can reap the benefits the cards can offer you. What you want is insight, a new perspective, or even just a reminder of what you already know but need to work on. This way, you'll be able to create a better future for yourself and those you love.

Using The Tarot When You're In A Relationship

Questions that revolve around love, marriage, divorce, and soulmates are things that clients come to me for quite often, so getting the most from your relationship reading is important. Whether you're reading for yourself or going to an experienced tarot reader, you don't want to end the session feeling disappointed or confused.

The most common mistake I see is when people hold back information or don't frame the question in a helpful way. Sometimes they're worried about what they might find out, so they aren't completely honest with their feelings, even to themselves. Other times, they're a bit skeptical and want to "test the cards" to see if the information is real and correct. The problem though is that it often results in inaccurate readings.

Let's say for example you want to know if your partner is cheating on you. You get your deck of tarot cards, shuffle them, and ask the question, "Is my partner seeing another woman?" As you can imagine, this will most likely result in a confusing reading because your partner probably sees other women all the time—coworkers, friends, and family. So, although the cards will let you know that he is, indeed, seeing one or more other women, it doesn't mean he's cheating.

Always be very specific with your questions. I've had clients who were so vague that I knew any information I got from the cards could be misinterpreted. I always say, general questions equal general answers, so you need to be crystal clear on what you really want to know. The reason is, that the cards can't be read correctly if you're holding back, asking too many questions, or not asking the right questions.

Let's say that you and your partner have become distant and you're just not happy in the relationship any longer. You're wondering what you should do. Stay and work through it or hope it will eventually all go away? Or break up? Rather than asking these simple yes or no questions, it's good to frame your query so that you're presented with helpful guidance and solutions. You could ask something like:

- What is the current energy in our relationship?

- What will happen if I stay in this relationship?

- What will happen if I leave the relationship?

- What things will change if I stay with them and what things will remain the same?

- How can we both be happy in this relationship?

- What can I do to help heal the relationship and become closer to them?

- How does my partner feel about our relationship?

- What is currently influencing my relationship?

- How can I help this relationship grow?

- What do I need to better understand about myself?

- What do I need to better understand about my partner?

- What is the potential outcome of this relationship and how does this happen?

- What issues do I need to work on to be a better partner?

Questions like these will give you the real answers you're looking for rather than something simple or, worse yet, confusing. You don't want to miss important information when you're trying to solve your love issues. That's why it's a good idea to focus on the big picture of your relationship rather than being hyper-focused on a straight yes or no answer.

How many questions you ask when reading the cards is up to you. I've found that between three and five is a good number. Any more and I tend to overwhelm myself. Before I do a reading I'll make a list of everything I want to know about my current problem or situation then choose the ones that are the most important. I'll then do the reading, take notes about the cards I got, and let that sink in for a bit. I know I can always go back to the tarot later in the day, tomorrow, or next week if I need more guidance or clarification.

The tarot is meant to offer guidance and direction, not to offer false hope and promises, or to scare and worry you. It's honest and unbiased. They're simply messengers, while you're the master of your life with free will. You always have the power to make your own decisions and choose your own course of action.

Why True Love Has Been Elusive

Whether you've recently gotten out of a relationship or have been single for a while, the tarot can help you find true love. I've had so many clients who wonder if they should just give up on ever finding a happy, stable relationship. They can't understand why they keep attracting the wrong type of person, even if they seem to have nothing in common. Or, they wonder why they've been alone and lonely for so long when they have so much love to give.

The truth is, finding a positive soulmate to spend the rest of your life with starts with ourselves. It's often hard to admit that we're the main reason love has been so elusive. Sure, a relationship could start off feeling like paradise, but without fail, it eventually feels more like a prison or a punishment. You stick it out as long as you can, sometimes far too long, and then you find yourself single and looking for love yet again.

Our outside world, especially our relationships, is a direct manifestation of our inside world. It seems logical then that a relationship that's happy and successful needs to start from within first and foremost.

The best relationships are when two people have:

- Discovered who they are are individuals.

- Have a strong sense of self.

- Are capable of expressing their feelings.

- Have set appropriate boundaries.

- Recognize their own needs and the needs of their partner.

- Are stable in their lives.

- When single, they can recognize traits in a potential partner that will or won't work.

When doing a tarot reading about love it's so easy to focus on who you might meet, where you could meet them and when, what they might be like and look like, and the energy that could be in the relationship. Almost always though, we fail to take into consideration our own belief systems, behavioral patterns, and more.

If you're serious about finding real and lasting love then it's best to start with yourself and ask the cards questions that will offer helpful answers. It's always a good idea to see what your current level of self-development is and how it could be influencing your love life. Regardless of the type of tarot spread you do, rather than asking, "When will I find love? What will they be like? Will I be happy?" and things of this nature, here are some more useful questions to ask:

- What areas do I need to work on to find true love?

- What's preventing me from finding my soulmate?

- What do I need to learn about myself that will make me a better partner?

- Where do I need to grow and heal so I can attract a positive partner?

- What patterns do I keep repeating that are influencing my love life?

- What are my true beliefs about love?

- What things do I need to change about myself?

- Where do I fail to honestly express myself?

- What do I need to do so that I'm open to real and lasting love?

- How will I feel when I meet this person/am with this person?

There are billions of people on this planet so there's no shortage of potential relationships. But if you consistently end up with the "wrong person" or are constantly looking for love but never find it, you honestly need to work on self-development and growth first. If not, you'll keep attracting the same type of partners you always have.

The tarot is a wonderful tool to help you explore your inner world and outer behaviors. Think of the cards as a mirror into your mind, heart, and soul, reflecting the truth back to you whether you're seeking guidance on love, money, health, or your career. They'll show you where you're most vulnerable and what's been standing in the way. It can help you discover influences and situations you might not even be aware of or believe had no lasting effect on you. This awareness helps you to become who you're truly meant to be. The more you learn about yourself and are aware of your patterns and behaviors the more you can change for the better and eventually meet the perfect person for you.

Using The Tarot To Find Your Soulmate

Your cards can help reveal what you're truly looking for in a relationship, what's preventing you from finding one another, where they might be, what they could be like, and many other details centered on love.

I believe we all have several soulmates throughout life. Some soulmates might be a friend, family member, or romantic partner that was only in our life for a short time. You can tell when someone is a soulmate because the connection is/was incredibly strong. When the timing is right and your souls are ready the two of you could be brought together to share the rest of your lives together.

It's not always sunshine and rainbows though. Many people believe that once you're with a soulmate life and love will be a breeze, you'll never argue, and you'll always feel wildly passionate for one another. The reality is, although soulmate relationships are, well, soul-deep, you're still two different people. You have your own upbringings, emotional baggage, thoughts, feelings, personalities, likes and dislikes.

The difference between a soulmate relationship and others that aren't is that the two of you are both committed to one another and the relationship. You want to be the best version of yourselves and to help each other do the same. Even if you do have occasional disagreements, you make amends quickly and get right back to those positive feelings. When you're with your soulmate you feel accepted and loved, and the good times far outweigh any of the bad.

Whether you believe people only have one soulmate or could have many—both romantic and platonic—the following spreads will help you find someone you have a soul connection with, as well as the energy and influences between the two of you and as individuals.

Is it really that easy to find your soulmate?

You lay out some tarot cards, get the information, and patiently wait for the Universe to do its thing and send love your way. In some ways, yes. Before that can happen though, you're going to have to work on yourself as we talked about in the previous section. If we don't do the inner work we need to so we can be our best selves, we'll just keep repeating the relationship patterns we always have.

That's not to say that you aren't good enough just as you are. What happens though is we don't realize that we've been attracting the wrong types of relationships because we're still carrying around hurt from the past. It's hard to have a healthy soulmate relationship when you're closed off, even if you want true love so badly.

We usually go through life and love blindly, following our feelings and subconscious programming. Instead, you can now become the type of soulmate you want to be. You can decide who and what you want for yourself, and a positive love will find you.

Now let's get to some love tarot spreads that will help you manifest your soulmate and guide the two of you together.

Before starting, make sure you feel relaxed and have released any thoughts or ideas about who or how your soulmate may be. You want your intuition to be the guide rather than any preconceived notions you might have about your true love.

Three Card Spreads

By now you already know how fond I am of these simple three-card spreads. I can get instant answers without a lot of other information to decipher and wade through. And, oftentimes, I'll start out with three cards and lay out others as my intuition guides me to do.

1. Relationship Overview Spread

This quick spread can help to bring you clarity and understanding of the type of relationship you want for the future. Or, it can help shed light on any relationship you've had in the past or even a present one. Shuffle your cards and lay out three of them which will represent:

Card #1 – You

Cards #2 – Your Soulmate

Card #3 – The Relationship

I like to lay the cards out side-by-side, but feel free to put them in any position you'd like. There's honestly no right or wrong way and I try not to be too stringent on card placement.

This is a good spread that gives you insight into the two of you and what type of energy could be in the relationship. While you're doing the reading and using your intuition and/or traditional meanings to interpret them, remind yourself that the cards are reflecting things as they are now. In other words, if nothing changes this is what you could expect from the relationship. If you see some information in the cards that worries or discourages you, remember that things can always change, especially if you put effort into it.

2. *When Will We Meet Spread*

The title of this spread is self-explanatory but it will offer you more information than just when the two of you will be brought together. While shuffling the cards, think about your soulmate and try to capture the feeling of how it would be to have them in your life. Lay out three cards that will represent:

Card #1 – Am I ready for love?

Card #2 – Are they ready for love?

Card #3 – When could we possibly meet?

This is such a good spread for really getting to know whether or not the two of you are ready, at this very point in time, for such a special relationship. You might have to do some more healing, they might, or the energies could be off at the moment for any number of reasons.

One client I did this reading for showed that she was ready but he wasn't. The reason didn't have anything to do with emotional or mental issues, but was instead geographical. His card showed that he lived in a completely different environment than she did. While she lived in a more lush, green area, his card showed a knight in the desert. Sure enough, she told me that was in the military and stationed in Afghanistan at the time. They did get together though when he got back to the States and they've been very happy ever since.

When I did this spread for myself years ago the cards showed that I wasn't ready and neither was my future partner. At the time, I still had three younger teenage daughters at home and I was very much wrapped up in being a single mom. The cards clearly pointed this out as well. With my potential partner, it showed that he was most likely going through a divorce or breakup. Although I wanted to be in a loving relationship, with those types of energies going on it would have been difficult to make things work smoothly. So, I patiently (and sometimes impatiently) waited.

3. Manifesting Your Soulmate Spread

For this spread, you'll be focusing on your relationship goal, the desired outcome. Rather than asking questions, you'll say out loud or in your mind, exactly what you're looking for in a soulmate relationship. Don't worry, you don't need to have a list of details, you can simply let your cards know that you want to find a partner who's a positive match for you and that the two of you can be happy in a long-term relationship. The key is to be specific with your intentions as you shuffle the cards and focus on what you want to manifest.

This spread is a little different because, after you shuffle the cards and think about what you want for your future, you'll go through the deck and choose one card for yourself and one for your future soulmate.

Don't think too hard as you look through the images and symbols. Allow your intuition to choose the cards that you feel represent you at your best and your partner at their best.

Now choose a card that represents your ideal life together. You're looking for the feelings in the card rather than something literal such as The Lovers, etc.

Also, don't feel obligated to choose only major arcana cards or cards with people in them. Trust that your higher self knows what you want and need and choose those cards. Lay them in front of you representing:

Card #1 – Your ideal self

Card #2 – Your ideal partner

Card #3 – Your ideal life together

When I say the word "ideal" in no way do I mean absolutely perfect. Nothing and nobody is perfect and striving for utter perfection is an unattainable goal that will just disappoint you and stress you out. In the sense of this reading, ideal means how you would feel happiest and most authentic.

Now that you have the cards in front of you, just look them over. Allow your mind to wander, sort of like a light meditation. To make this reading even more special feel free to light a candle, incense, put on mood music, lay out crystals, or whatever you'd like before you start.

Make sure you have your journal out to make notes on the messages in the cards. I always like to put the date, the cards I drew, and then my thoughts and impressions of them, along with any symbols that seem to call my attention. You never know what things in a card are going to pull at your senses. Don't second-guess yourself though.

After you do your reading, put everything away and just go about your day, allowing the energies of your reading to settle into your subconscious and ultimately manifest your relationship.

You might wonder if you should do this spread again or leave it as is. Some people will do this spread once a week and pull out the same cards to look over and meditate on. Others just let things unfold as they should and when they should. Still, others choose to do a reading once a week or once a month and allow their intuition to pull three other cards that feel right at the time.

We're always learning and growing, and life is always changing. It never hurts to check in and see where things are going. If you've been doing a lot of internal work or if things have changed a lot in your life, you'll most likely be drawn to another card that represents you and even possibly your future partner and your life together.

A good friend of mine had grown kids and was single for a few years. She was eager to be in a relationship again and did this manifestation spread. Six months later her life changed drastically. She ended up getting custody of her infant granddaughter and, obviously, wanted a man in her life who was okay with that. A few months ago she started talking to a man who had a three-year-old daughter and had custody of her 50% of the time. Before, my friend would have wanted someone without any young kids, but life can sometimes throw us curve balls. So, it's good to periodically check in with yourself and the cards to see if anything has changed or progressed.

4. About My Soulmate Spread

This is a 4-card spread to gather information about your potential partner and the energies surrounding the two of you. Shuffle your cards and lay four of them in front of you. You can either choose the top four cards or four random cards you pull from anywhere in the deck. The cards will represent:

Card #1 – What will my soulmate be like?

Card #2 – Under what conditions will I meet them?

Card #3 – What challenges will I need to overcome before meeting them?

Card #4 – What do I need to remember while on this journey of love?

As you've done in the other spreads, take notes and pay attention to the symbols, images, and potential messages. I'll be honest, this was my least favorite spread to do when I was looking for love because I felt, at least for me, I got too hung up on what my future partner might be like and where we could possibly meet. A lot of people find this spread helpful though. Give it a try and see how you feel about it though.

5. Is This My Soulmate Spread

This is a good reading if you're in a relationship, whether new or established, and want more information about it. This can help you to get closer to your partner, learn more about any challenges or obstacles you face, and the role you play in each other's lives. Shuffle your cards and lay out six cards. The cards will represent:

Card #1 – Is this person truly my soulmate?

Card #2 – How are we compatible or incompatible?

Card #3 – Why are they in my life? (Lessons you'll learn from them.)

Card #4 – Why am I in their life? (Lessons they'll learn from you.)

Card #5 – What issue(s) do we need to work on to become closer?

Card #6 – Potential outcome for our relationship.

This is a truly helpful reading though keep in mind that even if card #1 turns up in a reversed position it doesn't mean an automatic "no" answer. It could show where the two of you clash or an obstacle or issue that is making the relationship difficult. Yes, you can read the reversed card as a definite "no" if this feels right to you. Even if you read the message of the card of what the problem could be, it might be wise to ask yourself if it's something the two of you can overcome or want to work on.

When I did this reading for a client she got a reversed card in the "Is this person truly my soulmate?" position. It had three women on the card. Although she really liked this person, her intuition was telling her something wasn't quite right. A few months later she found out that he had never been in a serious relationship for more than half a year and tended to date a lot of women at once. She definitely didn't want to be in this type of relationship.

All of the spreads I just showed you can be packed with solid guidance and wisdom. Keep in mind though that as souls in human bodies relationships can often be complex. It's best to go into your tarot readings with an open mind and heart, but not get too stuck on anything you see in the cards. Yes, we should always be working to better ourselves for ourselves and the people we care about, but other than that it takes patience to let love happen and unfold as it should.

Additional Guidance And Direction

There are numerous books that center only on the traditional meanings of tarot cards so I'm not going to dive too deeply into that. Also, I hope that you'll work more intuitively with your cards so the messages and guidance are as helpful and as personal as possible. However, it's still nice to have something to go by, especially when you're first starting out or get stuck on a card and can't figure out what it's trying to tell you. Following, I give some information and brief definitions for the cards.

Reversed cards -

Keep in mind that when reading reversed cards it doesn't always mean something completely different or the exact opposite of what the upright meaning is. Instead, the card(s) could have appeared inverted as a way to:

- Get your attention

- Let you know that a challenge or obstacle might be more difficult

- An outcome or opportunity could be delayed

- It's something you've been putting off and now is the time to tackle it

I read reversed cards as well as upright, though some choose to only read cards in the upright position. The reason I choose to do both is I feel that when a card shows up reversed it's a sure sign that I need to work on the area more. Instead of having a separate meaning for a reversed card, it's simply a red flag saying that more attention and effort need to be applied in this area.

Other people might find it difficult to read a card when it's upside down or feel that it represents negative energy they simply don't want to deal with. That's completely okay, just read the cards in the way that feels right to you.

What's in the deck -

As we know, each of the 78 cards is filled with symbology and images that can offer us an endless amount of guidance and information. The first 22 cards, the Major Arcana, represent life's karmic and spiritual lessons. These are the bigger things in life as we go on our journey of self-awareness. Each card depicts the lessons and stages we encounter. That's why, if any come up in a reading, you know that the message is very important, down to a soul level.

The 56 other cards, the Minor Arcana, are the people, experiences, and challenges we face on a daily basis. These are issues that are temporary, lessons that are more minor and easier to work through, and just the positive and negative aspects of living life.

As you've seen, the Minor Arcana also has 16 Court Cards. Depending on the deck you have there are 4 Kings, 4 Queens, 4 Knights, and 4 Pages. These represent different personalities that we and others express.

The Minor Arcana is also divided into 40 cards (ace through 10) of 4 different suits. Again, depending on your deck, they're typically: Cups, Pentacles, Swords, and Wands. These represent various situations we encounter day to day.

Which interpretations to use -

When you lay out your card or cards and then look over these traditional meanings it might be confusing as to which definitions to use. I know when I first started out I wasn't sure what meaning to put to a particular card. I would ask my question, turn over the card, look at the explanation in the book, and then wonder which one was most fitting ... or most worrying!

This is why framing your question very concisely can be helpful, as well as using your intuition. Also, be sure to have an open mind and not put too much relevance on something in the interpretations that wouldn't really pertain to what you need guidance on at the moment.

Let's say you're in a new relationship, and feel a connection with this person, but perhaps you sense that something is slightly off but you aren't sure what it was. Now, I'm going to pull a card completely at random and see what it could point to. Using my Morgan Greer deck, I randomly pulled out the 3 of Swords. Using the example in the above paragraph, how could that pertain to this hypothetical situation?

Some standard interpretations are: A love triangle, someone interfering, miscommunication, arguments, delay, heartache, hurt feelings, minor surgery, unanswered questions, lack of focus or direction, and taking care of problems before they get worse.

It's easy to jump to conclusions and think that perhaps your partner is cheating. This is an awful place to be in when you have no proof or even a feeling that it might be happening because it can bring insecurities and suspicion to the forefront of your mind. Obviously, that could really ruin a relationship, especially if it isn't true. Or maybe you now believe they're going to have an operation you don't know about and you're suddenly worried about their health. Nobody needs that kind of stress, especially when there's not a shred of proof or even the slightest gut feeling that these things could be happening.

This is where having an open mind and focusing on your true needs and the guidance you're seeking comes in. Think about the relationship and ask if perhaps you do have some problems with communication, maybe you had an argument recently, or something has come up between the two of you and the cards are letting you know that it's a good idea to take care of it now rather than sweeping it under the rug. Or maybe there's a friend or family member who just keeps getting in the middle of your relationship and that's where "someone interfering" comes in.

Again, the tarot is about providing guidance regarding the questions you're seeking answers to. It's not about scaring you or making you feel worried about things that haven't even crossed your mind. It won't tell you something you don't already know or don't already suspect.

Have fun while learning -

If you're new to tarot it can seem overwhelming, but if you spend enough time with your cards, keep notes, and enjoy yourself rather than stressing about remembering the meanings too much you'll eventually feel much more comfortable with them. And, as I mentioned earlier in the book, the meanings can change depending on what's going on in your life at the time as well as the questions you ask.

Another thing that I've found interesting about the cards is I might interpret them one way and then when the situation has passed I look back and say to myself, "Oh, so that's what the cards were trying to tell me!" It's always a learning experience, no matter how long you've been reading.

Think of the tarot as a mirror of your soul and the key to inner peace, happiness, and wisdom. Every lesson you have gone through, are going through, or will go through can be found in the cards. When you consult them, you'll be shown what it is you need to work on. It's a much easier way to access your subconscious and find the wisdom and answers you're looking for.

Now let's get to some definitions of the cards. Again, this isn't everything you could ever learn about the cards. You can read ten different books and discover very different meanings. But, these are some of the most common interpretations and the ones I've used over the years.

Traditional Card Meanings

Major Arcana

0 - The Fool: Innocence, excitement, youthfulness, new energy, a new path, being a novice, learning from your lessons, ignorance, being more childlike, taking a leap of faith, learning from your past, brand new opportunity, a move (perhaps to another state).

1 - The Magician: Knowledge, self-control, intelligence, success, education, teaching others what you know, acquiring and using your skills, taking charge, taking action, determination, creativity, working your magic, speaking your mind, Mr. Right.

2 - The High Priestess: Awakening of intuition, wisdom, spirituality, secrets, stubbornness, learning, peace, letting go, psychic abilities, trusting your intuition, something hidden, supernatural events, Ms. Right.

3 - The Empress: Mother figure, Mother Earth, fertility, pregnancy, abundance, health, home life, moving to a new house, reaping your harvest, simplicity, doing things with your hands, crafts, hobbies, a new beginning.

4 - The Emperor: Father figure, ambition, stability, discipline, willpower, strength, stubbornness, opinionated, fearless, determination, following the rules, leadership, business owner, promotion.

5 - The Hierophant: Marriage, higher education, good advice, religion, your higher self, following tradition, blessings from above, searching for meaning, self-discovery.

6 - The Lovers: Your soulmate, love, sexual compatibility, emotional success, a tough decision, better times ahead.

7 - The Chariot: Triumph, success, driving passion, control, balance, revenge, travel, courage, power, opposites coming together, mode of transportation, reaching the finish line, road trip, moving forward.

8 - Strength: Inner strength, bravery, patience, health, courage, energy, self-discipline, brains over brawn, anger problems, winning someone over, a need to confront something or someone, finishing a tough project.

9 - The Hermit: A vision quest, solitude, healing, rest and relaxation, feeling introverted or shy, being cautious, needing a time out, a mentor or teacher, learning from your mistakes, letting go of the past, lighting the way for others.

10 - Wheel of Fortune: Personal journey, happiness, opportunity, positive new events, your luck is changing, a turn for the better, abundance, taking a gamble, a lucky break, a fresh start, something coming full circle.

11 - Justice: The legal system, truth, balance, control, signing legal documents, blind justice, fairness, things are in your favor, a decision being made, a debt being paid.

12 - The Hanged Man: Dark night of the soul, spiritual stagnation, self-sacrifice, holding yourself back, seeing the big

picture, seeing things from a different perspective, release, meditation, flexibility, dedication, a time of change.

13 - Death: Out with the old and in with the new, a new start, big changes, leaving something or someone behind, total transformation, seeing the light of a situation, end of a situation, need for a new direction. (*The tarot does not predict death!*)

14 - Temperance: Your guardian angel, moderation in all things, overindulgence, spiritual growth, need for better management, words of wisdom, patience, wise decisions, compassion, tranquility, peace, and harmony.

15 - The Devil: Being a slave to something or someone, addiction, abuse, being held back, jealousy, greed, sexual passion, a devilish prank, pessimism, anger, regrets, a negative person.

16 - The Tower: A wake-up call, being shaken up, a complete surprise, taking a fall, conflict, trouble at home, ruin that leads to renewal, quick or dramatic changes. (Though this sounds scary, I've experienced that it always leads to something better.)

17 - The Star: Following your dreams, goals, hopes, time of reflection, guiding light, bright future, good health, daydreaming, spiritual enlightenment, good things are on the way.

18 - The Moon: Important dreams, following your intuition, something that is hidden, your worries and fears, danger or phobia that is overcome, being a mediator, being stuck in the middle, secrets, gossip, confusion.

19 - The Sun: Happiness, freedom, positive relationship, engagement or marriage, success, birth, "yes!", feeling burned out, fiery energy propelling you forward, childlike fun, ultimate success.

20 - Judgment: A major decision, results of your choices, problems overcome, good or bad judgment, someone being too judgmental, paying debts.

21 - The World: Successful completion, traveling a long distance, soul growth that brings peace and harmony, what goes around comes around, freedom, relocation, karmic lessons learned/ completed.

Minor Arcana Meanings

In most decks, the Minor Arcana are divided into four suits:

<u>Wands</u>: This suit covers activities, social life, and career. It pertains to the spirit and those who are fire signs (Aries, Sagittarius, Leo). The season related to these cards is Spring.

<u>Cups</u>: These represent emotions, love, sensitivity, and pleasure. They pertain to emotions and water signs (Cancer, Pisces, Scorpio). The season related to these cards is Summer.

<u>Swords</u>: These are mental cards that involve thought, stress, and struggle. Swords point to the thought process and air signs (Libra, Aquarius, Gemini). The season related to these cards is Autumn/Fall.

<u>Pentacles</u>: These deal with the material world, health, finances, and property. These cover physical things and Earth signs (Taurus, Virgo, Capricorn). The season related to these cards is Winter.

There are four court cards in each suit:

King, Queen, Knight, and Page. These can represent people, stages in life, where you're at on a current path, aspects of your personality, or someone else's.

<u>Pages</u> can represent young people under the age of 20, those who act young for their age (whether positively or negatively), students of either sex, and people just starting on a new path. These people are usually interns or entry-level workers.

<u>Knights</u> can represent people in their 20s to early 30s, and those who are already on their path in life. These people are typically supervisors, managers, or starting their own businesses.

<u>Kings and Queens</u> are older people ages 35+ and/or those who are very established on their life path and/or good at what they do. They're typically business owners or higher up in the company they work for.

The Aces indicate the beginning of activity and the tarot cards that are numbered from 2 to 10 represent different aspects of your life: past, present, and future.

Wands

Ace of Wands - A new job, a new path, new ideas, starting a new business, sex, fertility, birth, excitement, eagerness.

2 of Wands - A choice, thinking things over, a partner, feeling restless, seeking something new, uncertainty, learning from your past.

3 of Wands - Taking a trip, asking for help, confidence, contemplation, adventure, courage, working hard for what you want, new ideas, an opportunity.

4 of Wands - Stability, happy home life, security, back to basics, socializing, peace and contentment, prosperity, positive energy.

5 of Wands - Struggle, competition, practice makes perfect, participation, disorganized, disagreements, proceeding with caution, pursuing your goals no matter what.

6 of Wands - Victory after a struggle, good news, the support of others, receiving recognition, hard work paying off, achievement, obstacles being overcome.

7 of Wands - Winning, overcoming problems, taking a stand, careful planning, communication, stable position, you are right, having strong convictions.

8 of Wands - Missing an opportunity, things happening quickly, taking immediate action, a message or letter, a fast ending, positive outcome, jealousy from others.

9 of Wands - Gathering strength, a long wait, defending a cause, responsibility, determination, protecting what's yours, the past haunting you, being careful of who you trust, being prepared, having patience.

10 of Wands - Success after a struggle, a great burden, over-extending yourself, too much pressure, too many responsibilities, the need to carry on no matter what.

Page of Wands - Being faithful, good news, having more fun, a new friendship, confidence, honesty, start of education or business, letting your ego get in the way.

Knight of Wands - Moving to a new house, starting a new job or career path, good ideas put into action, if you need to leave a situation now is the time.

Queen of Wands - Good in business, a friend, loyal, strong but loving female, a need for more socializing in your life, very responsible and caring, a tendency to worry too much.

King of Wands - Being clever and honest, receiving or giving good advice, self-employed, old-fashioned, dominant male, strong and honest leader.

Cups

Ace of Cups - The beginning of emotional happiness, a new love or rekindling of a relationship, new friendship, happiness, joy, contentment, fertility, peace, good health, receiving a gift.

2 of Cups - Emotional and spiritual love, feeling complete, emotionally balanced, romance, marriage, respect, understanding.

3 of Cups - Celebration, party, good friends, good news, an opportunity for growth, a problem being solved, a favorable outcome, a time of healing.

4 of Cups - Passing up opportunities, stress, boredom, depression, frustration, stagnation, afraid to try something new, taking time out, waiting for the right opportunity, self-doubt.

5 of Cups - Leaving something behind after an emotional investment, learning a lesson, being brokenhearted, letting go, turning your back on someone, loss of control, feeling ashamed, finding out something was untrue, releasing old beliefs.

6 of Cups - Someone from the past, childhood memories, a gift, friend or relative coming to visit, feeling nostalgic, enjoying simple pleasures, a new environment.

7 of Cups - Too many choices, feeling distracted, daydreaming, living in a fantasy world, seeking the best path, paying attention

to avoid mistakes, juggling too many things at once, taking the most solid choice.

8 of Cups - Putting the past behind you, a brave but difficult decision, surrender, completion, emotional growth, not letting pride get in the way, taking a new path that is slow to start, giving more than receiving.

9 of Cups - Wishes come true, feeling satisfied, weight gain, happy occasion, be careful of what you wish for, accomplishment, feeling comfortable, being rewarded for your efforts.

10 of Cups - Emphasis on home and family life, happy family, harmony, personal happiness, joint venture, achievement, contentment, community, paying close attention.

Page of Cups - Bright ideas, good news, feeling sensitive, new relationship, needing assistance, a good-hearted person, being too dependent, someone who will help you or you will help them.

Knight of Cups - Your soulmate, romance, creativity, imagination, a message of love, important notification of employment, an invitation, difficulty in saying no, getting distracted.

Queen of Cups - Psychic abilities, paranormal experiences, sensitivity, a visionary, mood swings, a good counselor, a loving female.

King of Cups – Receiving good advice or generosity from someone, being artistic, run by emotions, parental love, higher education/knowledge, great imagination.

Swords

Ace of Swords - Sex, triumph, a forceful attitude, new ideas, a card of victory, trusting in your own abilities.

2 of Swords - Making a decision, using logic, mental focus, a strong friendship, mutual respect, physical closeness.

3 of Swords - A love triangle, someone interfering, miscommunication, arguments, delay, heartache, hurt feelings, minor surgery, unanswered questions, lack of focus or direction, taking care of problems before they get worse.

4 of Swords - Taking a break, retreat, out of reach, solitude, rest and recovery, indecision and doubt, constant worrying, restless sleep, feeling lonely or isolated, gaining a new perspective.

5 of Swords – Consequences due to indecision, feeling betrayed or stabbed in the back, winning at all costs, tough competition, cutting your losses and letting go, don't let negative input influence you, the war is over.

6 of Swords - Crossing over to a better future, travel, relief from difficulties, trying to escape, physical separation from someone, a more positive time in life is ahead.

7 of Swords - Hard work and determination, refusing to take the easy way out, outside support, feeling tricked or robbed, seeing results of your labor.

8 of Swords - Frustration, confusion, disruption, unspoken jealousy, insecurity, feeling like a prisoner or trapped, not having enough information to make a decision, criticism, embarrassment, being overly cautious.

9 of Swords - Worry, nightmares or vivid dreams, headaches or migraines, insomnia, can't escape problems, broken promises, depression, a very stressful time, problems with the law.

10 of Swords - Back pain, illness, failure, immense stress, feeling overwhelmed, emotional isolation, the worst is nearly over, things will get better.

Page of Swords - Someone untrustworthy or jealous, immaturity, feeling paranoid, looking over your shoulder, a prankster, nervousness or anxiety, observing the actions of another.

Knight of Swords - Confrontation, competition, strategy, confidence, bravery, challenges, acting quickly, things are to your advantage, fighting over an issue.

Queen of Swords - Wisdom learned through pain, sharp mind and wit, seeking revenge, speaking before thinking, unresolved issues, misdirected anger, success is difficult though not impossible.

King of Swords – Critical man in authority, lawyer or law enforcer, a decision is final, having a harsh exterior, emotionally cold, intense focus on the task at hand, all work and no play, fairness.

Pentacles

Ace of Pentacles - A golden opportunity, improved finances, new job/raise/promotion, new skills leading to more money, a great time to start that project, excitement, clarity.

2 of Pentacles - Juggling finances, your ship coming in, finding balance, cutting back, managing your life better, be careful signing papers, credit approval, legal notice, an invitation, written communication.

3 of Pentacles - Being rewarded, receiving recognition, getting a certificate/diploma, making money through your skills, working long hours, self-employment, higher self-esteem.

4 of Pentacles - Saving money, being financially cautious, investing wisely, being greedy, being frugal, material indulgence, financial disputes, obstacles to getting what you want financially.

5 of Pentacles - Financial hardship, relationship problems, spiritual emptiness, physical ailment/injury, overdue bills, borrowing money, indecision, unnecessary spending, digging yourself out of debt.

6 of Pentacles - A helping hand, being generous, giving or receiving a gift, attending a party/event/seminar, letting money slip through your fingers, receiving unexpected money.

7 of Pentacles - Reaping what you sow, continue working on your projects, physical or financial stability after hard work, money can't buy happiness, having mixed emotions about a job or venture.

8 of Pentacles - Skilled in a craft or business, seeking or having specialized knowledge, success through hard work, job improvement, feeling bored with your job, possible promotion.

9 of Pentacles - Financially content, working from home, starting your own business, pleasurable home life, enjoying your career, achieving goals.

10 of Pentacles - Success achieved, family finances, family business, stable home life, financial security, peaceful surroundings, family gathering or reunion, securing your home.

Page of Pentacles - A physically attractive person, going back to school, studying for a career, learning something new, ambition and drive, management skills, being materialistic, exciting news, using common sense, a short-term relationship that's purely physical.

Knight of Pentacles - A dependable and responsible person, military or security guard, someone you can trust, need for planning and organizing, accountant/banker/investor, assistance and protection, perseverance pays off.

Queen of Pentacles – An artistic or creative person, generosity, intelligence, good listener, loyalty, security, being protective, sticking to a budget, debt reduction, a down-to-earth person, enjoying the comforts of life, positive financial outcomes.

King of Pentacles – Financial stability, business owner, higher up in a company, spending money on material items, excellent mix of money and love in a person, having a connection, a selfless and generous person.

Number Meanings

When you're doing a reading pay attention to any numbers that repeat themselves, either in the current reading, or if the number(s) keeps showing up in subsequent readings as well. They're incredibly helpful for a bit of extra guidance, showing what your current strengths and weaknesses are, and where you might need to work on something. Just like tarot interpretations, there are many books and websites dedicated to numerology that go into detail so feel free to do some more exploring on your own.

Most recently, I kept getting several number 8s in my readings. Besides the tarot definitions of all the cards I drew, I knew that that the number 8 was important. Yes, it could pertain to a time frame of say 8 weeks, 8 months, etc. but I also knew the number itself held a message.

Looking at the meanings, I saw that the number 8 could represent: Unity, power, leading, materialism, confidence, compromise, letting go of control.

My question was, "How can I feel less anxious in life?" The number 8 came up a few times so I knew the message was important. Looking over the definitions I saw right away which one pertained to me and my situation: "letting go of control". Due to the trauma in my childhood and a few relationships, I always strive for total control. Of course, that's a very stressful way to live. Trying to control everything or everyone is a no-win situation. So, it was another reminder from the tarot of what I needed to work on.

Meanings of numbers

1 - Leadership, independence, confidence, individualism, power, courage, resilience in life, overthinking.

2 - Compassion, determination, partnership, balance, flexibility, trust, opening your heart.

3 - Attraction, extroversion, communication skills, creativity, imagination, relating to others on a deeper level.

4 - Stability, logic, loyalty, work, building, consistency, determination, patience, organization, being flexible with changes.

5 - Adaptability, adventure, exploring, versatility, curiosity, selfishness, finding your life purpose.

6 - Protective, selflessness, service, support, harmony, tranquility, romance, home

and family, personal comfort, self-care.

7 - Thoroughness, personal beliefs, logic, self-analysis, meaningful relationships

8 - Unity, power, leading, materialism, confidence, compromise, letting go of control.

9 - Integrity, acceptance, wisdom, teaching, communication scale, diversity, doing what you love.

10 – With this number, I usually read it to mean that a situation has reached an end and a new cycle will begin—usually for the better!

Four Common Obstacles

Anyone who owns a deck of tarot cards can learn to do readings for themselves, and even others. The cards hold so much potential for personal growth and insight into your inner and outer world. No matter how eager you are to read the cards, you might find that trying to interpret them, especially when it comes to your love life, things just aren't happening the way the cards said they would. Or, when looking them over during a reading, you feel overwhelmed, lost, or confused. There are a few reasons this happens so let's talk about them.

1. Not Being Objective.

When reading for ourselves it's far too easy to see what you want most or fear most in the cards. In order to get the most guidance from your deck you need to be able to take a step back and read the cards objectively. If you always feel that reading for yourself is difficult because you're too close to the situation, the simple solution is to simply pretend you're doing a reading for someone else.

I do this often and even word things in the third person. "Kelly wants to know what she can do to become closer to her partner. Kelly needs guidance on the things keeping her from finding true love." This almost always works.

When reading for yourself, it's easy to contradict or deny what the cards are trying to tell you. This is especially true if we see something potentially negative or unflattering in the reading. You don't want to admit these things so you ignore the message or lay out a few more cards for "clarification". Instead, just pretend you're reading for another person and try to be as unbiased and open-minded as possible.

2. Being Skeptical.

Another huge obstacle that can prevent you from reaping the rewards that the tarot offers is not believing how helpful these cards can be in transforming your life. Some people are skeptical because of religious reasons, although a part of them is curious which is why they're trying the tarot at all. Then there are others who believe the cards are worthless when it comes to helpful messages and see them just as interesting works of art. And some just can't believe that a set of cards can be so telling and helpful.

If you think about it, it is logical to believe that a seemingly simple deck of cards can't possibly hold so much wisdom and direction that can potentially change your life and answer all of your questions. That's why it's good to remind yourself that the imagery on the cards helps to tap into your higher self and subconscious, bringing out information you already know or suspect. There's really nothing mystical about it.

3. Being Afraid.

Even if someone is curious about the tarot and bought a deck, it's still common for many people to find the messages, or even some of the artwork, frightening. They might look at the cards and see their worst fears in them, especially if they get what they consider to be "scary" cards such as Death and The Devil.

Although they're fascinated, even momentarily, by the tarot, they often stick their cards away and think they're evil or that negative things will start happening in their lives.

Whenever anyone worries and asks me questions about this, I tell them to relax and know that the tarot cannot predict death, it can't make bad things happen, and it doesn't tell you things you don't already know. Yes, a lot of information the tarot shares with us focuses on our subconscious or things we don't want to face, but it can't tell you something you aren't already aware of in some part of your mind or soul.

Mostly, it shows you what you need to work on and be more aware of. It also offers guidance and direction to help you reach your goals and dreams. It can even show you where you consistently get stuck and how to overcome that. Tarot cards are your friends, not harbingers of doom and destruction.

4. Being Impatient.

When first starting to read the tarot it can be a bit disheartening when you want to understand it and perfect it right away. This is just one of the reasons why I love reading the tarot intuitively—anyone can do it and they can do it immediately. A lot of things can get in the way to trip you up though, such as second-guessing your instincts, worrying too much, seeing what you hope most or fear most in the cards, and being impatient with the guidance and messages.

Give yourself time to really get to know your cards. I gave you some exercises earlier in the book that will really help, and I offer more in my other book *Intuitive Tarot – Read The Tarot*

Instantly. It's like the difference between looking at a friend and a complete stranger. When you see your friend things are familiar and you can gauge their emotions by their body language, voice tone, the look on their face, etc. Whereas with a stranger, everything is new and unknown.

There's also impatience when it comes to the happening of things. We really want to find a wonderful partner, fall in love, and live happily ever after *right now.* Or, we want to get out of our current negative situation ASAP. Although the cards can offer a general time frame, since we're humans, have free will, and other factors are involved in our lives, the timing might not go along as the cards initially predicted. And that's okay!

I'm a firm believer in the fact that things happen when they should. Sometimes they happen more quickly, sometimes a lot more slowly, and sometimes it seems that nothing will happen at all. When I get frustrated I remind myself that the information I got from the reading will happen when it should. Maybe I need to make some changes to help move things along. Maybe there are things outside of my control. Maybe I'm not ready for this change or opportunity just yet so I've subconsciously blocked it.

Each one of these obstacles is as easy or difficult to overcome as we allow them to. I always tell friends and clients to be patient with themselves. Life didn't get to where it is overnight, your beliefs could run deep, and problems or current situations could be difficult, so take things one step at a time and keep working with your cards. The rewards are well worth it.

Contact Me/Book A Reading

Whether your problems or concerns are in the areas of love, finances, family, career, health, education, or your path in life, I offer professional psychic counseling, caring guidance, and solutions that work!

I use no tools. Instead, I'll connect directly with your higher self and your spirit guides to help you through any situation and achieve the best possible results. No problem is too big or too small, and your questions will be answered in detail.

I'll let you know absolutely everything that comes through in the reading which typically includes past, present, and future energies, guidance, time frames and predictions. Your guides may also include information on an important past life, aura energy, soul symbols, and more. Each reading is in-depth, filled with positive energy and guidance, and includes one free clarification email.

All readings are done via email. By offering my readings through email you'll be able to save your reading and go back to it again and again for guidance.

I look forward to reading for you!

D[1]rKellyPsychic.com

---

1. http://psychicreadingsbydrkelly.webs.com/psychic-readings